IN THE
NEWSROOM

D1716803

Anna watches tapes of an event
she reported on earlier that day.

APRIL
KORAL

# In the Newsroom

PHOTOGRAPHS BY
CARL GLASSMAN

A FIRST BOOK
FRANKLIN WATTS
NEW YORK I LONDON I TORONTO
SYDNEY I 1989

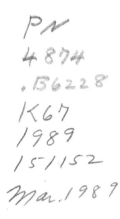
Photographs courtesy of:
AP/Wide World Photos: pp. 17, 20;
UPI/Bettmann Newsphotos: pp. 26, 39.
All other photographs by Carl Glassman.

Library of Congress Cataloging-in-Publication Data

Koral, April.
In the newsroom / by April Koral; photographs by Carl Glassman.
p.      cm.—(A First Book)
Summary: Describes what goes on in the newsroom of a television
station by following Anna Bond, reporter/anchor for Channel 4 in New
York City, through a typical day.
ISBN 0-531·10463-X
1. Television broadcasting of news—Juvenile literature. 2. Bond,
Anna. [1. Television broadcasting of news. 2. Occupations.]
I. Glassman, Carl, ill. II. Title III. Series.
PN4874.B6228K67 1989
070.1'9—dc19                                              87-25178    CIP    AC

TO MOTHER
AND DAD
A.K.

"I'm basically a nosy person. I like asking questions. That's why I became a reporter."

Anna Bond,
TV news reporter

The St. Louis Cardinals played the Los Angeles Dodgers tonight. What was the score?

The president made an important speech this morning. What did he say?

You heard that your teachers may go on strike. Is it true?

You're going swimming tomorrow. Will it rain?

Turn on the TV news and find out.

Every day millions of Americans tune into morning, evening, or late night news shows to hear—and see—what is happening around town and around the world. Most television stations have teams of reporters and camera crews who "cover" the news of their city. In New York City, Anna Bond is a reporter for Channel 4's evening news. This is the story of how she does her job.

Anna lives in a large apartment house in New York City. Every morning, before work, she feeds her daughter and plays with her. Then she has breakfast and reads the newspaper. She often cuts out articles that interest her. One day she might want to do a story on the same subject.

At home Anna reads the newspaper. She cuts out articles on topics that interest her and that she might report on someday.

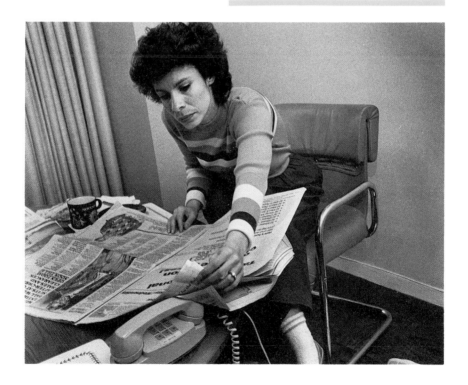

Anna works in the borough of Manhattan, from which a never ending
stream of interesting news comes.

Anna has always liked to write and was a reporter for
her high school newspaper. She studied broadcasting at
Queens College in New York City, where she helped to
start a radio station. After graduating, Anna was hired by
Channel 7. She worked hard and did many other jobs at
the TV station before she became a reporter. Later, she

moved to Houston, Texas, to work as an **anchor.** Anchors read the news and introduce stories covered by other reporters. Two years later, Channel 4 in New York City offered her a job as reporter and anchor. It promised to be a challenging and exciting job and Anna accepted it. Now, she and her husband, Gary Mason, a Houston eye surgeon, fly across the country several times a month to see each other.

Anna's workday begins at 3:30 in the afternoon. She walks the twenty blocks from her apartment to the Channel 4 offices, which are across the street from Radio City Music Hall in midtown Manhattan. Anna takes the elevator to the seventh floor and goes to the newsroom, which is bustling with activity. Everyone is getting ready for the early evening news show, and the air is filled with the sound of clacking typewriters. Anna's desk is at one end of the room. It is cluttered with books, papers, a stack of fan letters, a dictionary, several newspapers, a calendar, and dozens of letters from people and organizations who have ideas for stories they want Anna to cover.

After hanging up her coat, Anna heads for the desk of Jeff Greene, the evening **assignment editor.** While she waits for him to finish his conversation, she reads a newspaper.

Jeff has one of the most important—and busiest—jobs in the newsroom. He decides with the **producer**

An overview of the newsroom

which stories will appear on the evening news. On his desk are four telephones (on which he can receive fifteen different calls at one time!) and a two-way radio. He uses the radio to talk to reporters and camera crews when they are in different parts of the city covering a story. He also has a police and fire "scanner" radio.

Emergency calls for police and firefighters come in over the scanner. If Jeff overhears the police talking about a big fire or about a bank robbery that's taking place, for example, he will quickly send a reporter and camera crew to the scene. If possible, he will try to get them there before the other TV stations' crews arrive. Behind Jeff are three TV sets tuned to channels 2, 4, and 7. Throughout the night, Jeff keeps an eye on which stories the "competition" is covering.

Jeff's desk is a clutter of telephones, papers, and radio scanners.

Everyone keeps an eye on the news broadcasts of the other channels.

Although he never leaves the newsroom, Jeff is a reporter. People sometimes call him to tell him about an event, or about a problem in their community that deserves attention. He might also phone the police to find out if any arrests have been made in a recent murder case or call a hospital to learn the condition of a patient who is in the news. No wonder Jeff likes to call his desk ''the newsroom's window on the world.''

Jeff and Anna look at the news stories that have come over the wire service machines. The **wire ser-**

**vices** have reporters working all over the world. Their stories are sent electronically to machines that are in hundreds of television and newspaper newsrooms. Thanks to the wire services, television and newspapers can cover news stories in many countries without ever having to send their own reporters there. The wire services also have reporters stationed in New York City and other large cities around the United States.

Jeff and Anna look over news wire reports.

"There's nothing much here," Jeff says, as he looks over the stories about New York City. "What about a story on the fish market workers who are going on strike tonight?"

"Is the fish market open now?" Anna asks, turning to editor Jim Unchester.

"No," says Jim, or "Unch," as everyone calls him. "It's only open early in the morning."

"I don't think that would be good then," Anna says. "We won't be able to get any good shots."

**Shots,** or pictures, are very important to a TV news story. Are the shots interesting? Will they keep an audience's attention? Will the viewer turn to another channel? These are some of the questions TV news editors ask themselves every day.

"I guess you're right," Jeff says to Anna.

"That fire is still going on in Brooklyn," Unch says to Jeff.

"Do we have a shot of it?"

"Yes," Unch says. "A camera crew is down there now."

The camera crew's van has an antenna on its roof that can send pictures to a receiver in Manhattan. The receiver, which looks like a big dish, is on top of the Empire State Building. From there, it goes by underground cable to the newsroom.

Jeff presses a button below one of the TVs, and a picture of a boat appears on the screen.

"Where's the fire?" Jeff asks.

"You can't see it," explains Unch, who has been talking by two-way radio to the cameraman who is there. "It's in the bottom of the boat."

Fires are among the most reported news events.

"Well, we can't have a reporter stand in front of the camera and say, 'There's a fire in this boat, but you can't see it,' " Jeff says.

They decide not to send Anna there.

Anna returns to her desk and calls a friend. Meanwhile, other reporters are getting their stories ready for the six o'clock news. At the desk next to her, David Diaz has just come back from covering the funeral of a girl who was murdered.

"Was it horrible?" Anna asks. David silently nods his head.

Some reporters see so much tragedy that it is hard for them to be shocked. Critics of television news say that there should be fewer stories about murders, fires, and accidents. These stories may attract people's attention, but they fail to show the whole picture of what's happening in a community or city.

On the other side of Anna's desk, a woman is setting up a camera. A story about a trial will be on the news tonight. Since cameras are not allowed in the courtroom in New York, an artist drew sketches of the witnesses who took the stand. Before these sketches can be shown on TV, they must be shot on videotape. Becky Jansch, the camerawoman, has pasted the sketches on the wall and is videotaping each of them.

After she's finished, Anna stops to talk to her. She wants to compliment her on her camerawork for a recent

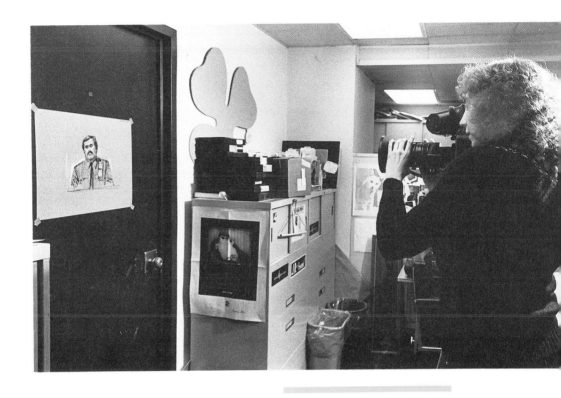

Becky Jansch shoots a picture
of an artist's sketch of a witness
testifying in a trial. Cameras are
not allowed inside the courtroom.

story they did together. Anna is in the middle of describing the shot she liked best when Jeff's voice comes over the loudspeaker. He sounds serious. "We have a report that there's a fire on a train in a tunnel in Queens. There might be injuries."

Firemen rescuing people from a burning
building makes for dramatic film footage.

While working as a TV reporter, Anna has covered many fires. A few years ago, she was sent to a fire in Manhattan. Fires are often out by the time the TV cameras arrive. This one was not. When Anna and the camera crew stepped out of their van, they saw firemen hurriedly giving artificial respiration to people who had been trapped inside a burning building.

"The firemen were heroes," Anna recalls, ". . . but nine men died." Anna went back to the office and spent the whole afternoon **editing** the tape. The story ran for three minutes on the news that night—an unusually long time for a television news story. It was also so well done that Anna won an Emmy Award for her work.

Using the loudspeaker, Jeff calls the name of another reporter to cover the fire story. Anna picks up the phone when suddenly the voice of Jeff Greene fills the newsroom again. "Anna Bond, please. Anna Bond." Anna quickly puts down the phone and hurries over to Jeff's desk.

"I'm sending you on the second part of the story," he tells her. "Go to the Queens Plaza station where the trains have stopped. There are a lot of people who can't get home. See what's happening and what they're going to do."

Anna grabs her pocketbook, notebook, and pen.

"The crew will meet you downstairs," Jeff says as she's halfway out the door.

Outside the building, a camera crew is waiting for Anna in a van. As they drive, they listen in on a conversation on the two-way radio.

"I hit a pothole and busted my oil pan." It's the voice of a courier. Couriers drive the videotape back to the newsroom after the cameraperson is finished shooting. This courier is supposed to deliver the tape for the first part of the story on the fire. "I've plugged it up but I'm going to have to stop for more oil."

The voice from the newsroom sounds worried. "They need that tape for the six o'clock show."

"Don't worry," the courier says. "It won't take me long. Maybe five minutes."

But it's 5:15 already.

The car inches its way through rush-hour traffic. Outside, the streets are busy with Christmas shoppers and the trees are glowing with holiday lights. But Anna hardly notices them. Her eyes are on a small clock on the car's dashboard. The minutes are ticking by and the car is moving very slowly.

Suddenly, Jeff's voice comes over the two-way radio. "Three-two to Anna Bond, Anna Bond."

Anna picks up the radio. "Three-two. This is Anna Bond for Jeff Greene. What's happening?"

"Anna, I'm going to call you off this story. The situation seems to have calmed down. They've put the fire out and the trains will be running again soon."

Anna listens to a conversation on
the two-way radio in her news van.

Anna leans back in the seat. "I was beginning to look forward to doing this," she says with a sigh.

When Anna gets back to the office, the hallway is lined with teenagers who have come to watch the taping of the "Late Night with David Letterman" show.

"Hey, there's Anna Bond," a boy says as she walks by. Anna doesn't mind when strangers say hello to her. "It's flattering," she says. "It means people are listening and responding to me. That's what communication is all about."

In the newsroom, Jeff and a handful of other editors are watching the six o'clock news. Channel 7's first story is about the train fire. "They got it," Jeff says, as he sees Channel 7's pictures of the fire. He feels bad that by the time Channel 4 got the tape, it was too late for the six o'clock news.

Jeff turns his back to the TV screens and talks to Anna.

"The Brooklyn Academy of Music is showing a new ballet tonight in honor of the one hundredth anniversary of the Brooklyn Bridge. Before the ballet, there's going to be a party and Mayor Koch and the last three mayors of New York will be there. The party starts at seven."

Anna nods her head and goes to the desk of Janet Paist, the producer for the evening news. Janet decides how long each story will be and where it will go in the show.

"How long are you planning for this story?" Anna asks Janet. Janet is busy working on putting together the eleven o'clock news show and barely has time to lift her head. "A minute and a half," she says.

Janet Paist is the producer for the evening news. She decides how long each story will be and when it will be shown during the program.

Feature stories usually focus on the less dramatic, quieter events taking place in a community, such as commemorations of anniversaries and birthdays. The birthday party for the Brooklyn Bridge, however, was so dazzling it outstaged all the genuine news stories of the day.

Janet knows that she can't give too much time to any one story because there are only nineteen minutes and fourteen seconds in the half-hour news show. The rest of the time is commercials. And since she must include four minutes of sports and two minutes of weather, she doesn't have much time for the rest of the news. So every second counts!

Tonight, Anna is going to do a **feature story.** A feature is a story with "human interest." It may be about a party where there are many famous people or an animal shelter that is looking for families to adopt a pet or a school with the best students in the city. A **news story** is different from a feature. It is about important events that have just happened.

Anna meets the camera crew downstairs, and they drive across the East River to Brooklyn, which is one of

Anna reads a magazine article about the Brooklyn Bridge to prepare herself for her upcoming interviews.

the five "boroughs" that make up New York City. In the near darkness of the van, Anna reads a magazine article about the Brooklyn Bridge's approaching birthday.

The party has already begun by the time Anna and the crew arrive, and a red carpet has been rolled out on the sidewalk in front of the Brooklyn Academy of Music. One limousine after another stops to let off its elegantly dressed passengers. Anna's crew tonight is Jim Pich, the cameraman, and Jim Zoltowski, Jr., an **audio technician** who records the interviews and other sounds. They stand next to the curb along with the camera crew from Channel 7. All of them are on the lookout for the four mayors. That's who their TV audience will want to see.

As they wait, Jim Pich is thinking about his camera battery. When was the last time he changed it? It's cold outside, and low temperatures shorten the life of the battery. Finally, former Mayor Robert Wagner steps out of a limousine. Jim quickly throws the lights on him and the cameras roll. Unfortunately, the ex-mayor is walking into the building with his back to the cameras. But Jim is not shy. "Mayor," he shouts. "Mayor, give us a wave." Mayor Wagner turns around. "How are you doing?" he says, as the cameras roll again. "You're looking good," Jim says, finishing taping.

Meanwhile, Anna is interviewing Pamela Pettinella, who helped organize the party. "Who built the bridge?"

Former New York City mayor Robert Wagner
stops briefly to talk with reporters.

Anna asks her. "How long did it take to build?" "Does it
need many repairs?" As Anna speaks to Pamela and the
two camera crews talk to each other, another former
mayor, John Lindsay, comes around the corner and
walks into the building without anyone noticing him.

Anna and the crew go inside to the party. The room
is noisy and crowded and there is hardly enough space
for Anna and the crew to walk around in. Jim Zoltowski is

worried about the band, which is very loud. He wants to be sure to get the clearest possible sound when Anna does her interview.

"Where is Mayor Lindsay?" Anna asks Pamela, who looks around the room and points to him. Anna goes up to him. "What do you think of when you think of Brooklyn?" she asks him. Not surprisingly, he says he thinks of the Brooklyn Bridge. Anna asks him a few more questions and, in less than a minute, the interview is over.

"Has Mayor Koch come yet?" Anna asks Pamela. "Not yet," she tells her. "I have to get him," Anna says, a little worried. The ballet is going to start soon and then it will be too late to speak to him. She goes into the lobby, but in a few seconds she dashes back into the room—almost tripping over some of the guests. She heads for the camera crew. "The Mayor. He's here. He's here!"

The camera crew comes to life and rushes to the door. The moment Mayor Ed Koch steps into the room, Anna plants herself in front of him, and the camera lights flood both of them. The microphone is already a few inches from his face. "Hello, Mr. Mayor," she says. The mayor smiles. He's used to reporters stopping him wherever he goes. He also knows Anna; she's interviewed him many times. She asks him a few questions, thanks him, then heads for the theater.

Anna interviews New York's
current mayor, Ed Koch.

As Anna walks toward the theater, a man says to his wife: "There's the lady from the news." The woman stops Anna. "I watch you every night from my bed," she tells her, smiling happily.

Anna and the crew go up to the balcony of the theater. Jim takes out one of the seven microphones he carries with him. This one is called a **shotgun micro-**

**phone,** and it is used to pick up sounds that are far away. He points it toward the orchestra. While he records the music, Jim Pich tapes the ballet. Anna watches the dancers, but her mind is on the story she is going to write.

As Anna watches the ballet, she is also thinking about the story she is going to write.

After ten minutes, they quietly leave the theater. In the office downstairs, Anna calls Jeff. "We're going to the Brooklyn Bridge now to do some taping," she tells him.

There's silence on the other end of the phone. Then Jeff says: "That doesn't leave you much time to edit."

"Don't worry," Anna answers.

The camera crew loads the equipment into the van and they head for the Brooklyn Bridge. At the foot of the bridge, Anna and the crew get out of the van. Anna and the cameraman had been planning to tape the bridge from here, but they decide that it would be more dramatic if they were in the middle of the bridge.

They find the footpath and start walking.

It's a quarter of a mile to the middle of the bridge, and Anna finds it hard to walk in her high-heeled shoes on the wooden path. When they stop, Jim Zoltowski hands her the microphone. Anna is going to talk a little about the history of the bridge. She wrote the words in the theater and memorized them on the way here in the van.

The cars are rumbling beneath them. "Can you hear me?" she asks Jim. He asks her to hold the mike closer to her mouth. "Okay now," he says. The cameraman is also concentrating very hard. It is dark, and he must make sure that Anna is in focus. He also notices that the

Cars rumble loudly beneath her as Anna
talks about the history of the Brooklyn Bridge
while her cameraman tapes her.

footpath is shaking a little from the traffic below. It's not easy to keep the 20-pound (9-kg) camera steady.

After Jim has finished taping, Anna runs the long way back to the foot of the bridge. A courier is waiting for the tape to take back to the newsroom. When she gets into the car, she looks at the dashboard clock. "It's not 9:20 already, is it?" she asks. The story must be ready for the eleven o'clock news.

Anna doesn't waste time as they drive uptown. Her lips move silently as she practices the opening lines of her story—when the viewer will hear her voice but not see her face. That's called the **voice-over.**

It's 9:40 when Anna reaches the seventh-floor offices. She walks quickly to the newsroom. As it gets later, Anna feels more and more nervous. But she also likes the excitement of the approaching deadline.

Anna goes to the desk of Terry Raskyn, the associate producer. Terry's job is to write the **script** for the anchor and the introductions to the reporters' stories.

"What do you have?" she asks Anna.

Anna describes what the story is about. Together, they write a few short sentences. Terry tries to make these introductions "ear-catching," she says, so that the viewer will be curious and want to keep watching the show. Anna also gives Terry the **supers** that she has typed. They are the words on the bottom of the TV screen that identify who is talking.

It's almost 10:00 P.M. when Anna arrives at the **editing room.** In this small room, there are two TV screens and dozens of lights, switches, and levers. Ed Smith, who is waiting for Anna, knows what each of them is for. He is the tape editor.

Anna and Ed Smith, the tape editor, begin editing the tapes.

Editing a story is probably the most difficult part of a TV news reporter's job. The cameraman has shot a lot of tape, and the audio technician has recorded many interviews. But Anna cannot use everything. She will have to decide: Which shots are the best? Which help tell the story? Which interview is the most interesting?

Before she starts to edit, Anna reads the voice-over, which she has practiced in the car, into a microphone while Ed records it. Although the voice-over is only ten seconds long, Anna wants it to be perfect. "Let me do it again," she says to Ed after she's finished. She reads it once more under her breath, crosses out a line, and adds some new words. "Okay, I'm ready," she says.

After recording the voice-over again, Anna and Ed start editing. On the left screen is the unedited tape. Ed plays the beginning. As Anna watches it, she looks at the numbers—called a **time code**—at the bottom of the screen. When a part of the tape she wants to use appears on the screen, she writes down the numbers.

Anna decides to start the story with a shot of the Brooklyn Academy of Music. Then she will show the guests arriving in their limousines.

"Go to 31–57," she says to Ed, referring to the time code. Ed rewinds the tape. She looks at it again. "It's boring. There are no people in the picture," she complains.

Anna decides to show the building for only five seconds. "Let's get in and out fast," she tells Ed, meaning that she wants it to be on the screen only a very short time. Ed presses several buttons, and the section of the tape that Anna wants is now "set" on the second screen. Next, she asks Ed to play the tape of the guests arriving. Ed stops the tape as a woman in an evening gown steps out onto the red carpet. "No," Anna says, "keep going. We have a better shot." Finally, they find the one Anna remembers.

Ed presses some more buttons and puts these shots onto the tape on the right screen. He plays the tape on the right screen with the shots of the building and the arriving guests. Together, it is exactly ten seconds long. Anna's voice-over will fit perfectly.

"Let's go to the first sound bite," Anna says to Ed. A **sound bite** is an interview. One of the mayors is speaking. He has just said a few sentences and is pausing for breath when Anna says "Out!" Ed stops the tape. Anna has to interrupt the mayor. She can give him only ten seconds to speak.

As they continue working, cameraman Jim Pich comes in to watch. After they finish, Ed replays the tape on the right screen. "It's one-thirty on the nose!" Anna says proudly. In other words, it is one minute and thirty seconds long—just what Janet wanted. She glances at the clock on the wall. It is 10:40.

Even the comments of the mayor of New York get cut short to fit them into a news time slot.

Anna goes back to the newsroom. She puts a piece of paper in the typewriter and types up the **tape page,** which tells at what time the different interviews appear in the story. A technician will then be able to put the supers on the screen at the right time. She gives the tape page to Terry. Anna's story will be the **kicker**—the last story on the show.

It's after 11:00 P.M. when Anna leaves the office. As she walks home through the nearly empty streets, she thinks of the two million people who are looking and listening to her on their television sets. And she's glad she did a good job.

"People don't just want to hear the news. They want to hear it from someone they like . . . someone they feel comfortable with."

Anna Bond, anchor

On weekends, Anna Bond is anchor on the evening news.

Today is Sunday, and every Sunday Anna meets one of her friends for a game of tennis. Anna also takes exercise classes. "It's important to stay healthy," she says. "It makes you look better, which is important when you're on TV."

At 3:30 P.M., her friend drives Anna to her office. In the newsroom, Anna stops to talk to the weekend news producer, Stephan Cohen. He gives her a story from the wire service about the state legislature. It is much too long to read on the air. Anna's job is to shorten it so that she can read it in thirty-five seconds!

Even though it is so short, Anna works for a long time on the story. A good TV news story must be very clearly written so that the TV listener can understand every word. And to make sure that it's the right length, Anna uses the stopwatch she keéps in her drawer.

Meanwhile, down the hall from the newsroom, Don Gould, the sports anchor, and Dave Katz, the sports producer, are watching one basketball game and two football games—all at the same time.

To make sure stories are the right length, Anna always keeps a stopwatch handy.

Sports reporters watch as many games as they can and read about what they can't watch. Many sports fans do this without getting paid!

"Great play!" Don says.

"Yeah, nice shot," Dave agrees. "Too bad you couldn't see the ball go into the basket."

Dave spends many hours looking for the best—or the worst—plays of the game. He writes down the time and a brief description of each of them. Don then chooses the most interesting and replays them on the air. Since Don and Dave cannot watch *all* the games, Don also reads the wire service reports about the games and the scores.

Being a sports anchor is a great job, says Don, who used to be a radio disc jockey, but one that also has its disadvantages. "I can't really enjoy watching a game at home," he says. "I'm always thinking about which plays to put on the air."

Back in the newsroom, Ralph Penza, who is anchoring with Anna tonight, is having a discussion with Stephan Cohen. They are talking about the show's first sto-

Ralph Penza, Anna's co-anchor for the show, talks with weekend news producer Stephan Cohen about the lead story.

ry, or **lead.** The lead should be the most important event in the news. What was today's most important event? Ralph and Stephan disagree.

Stephan is planning to open the show with a story about Barney Clark, the man who had an artificial heart implant.

"That's a weak lead!" Ralph says. "Nothing is new except that his doctors are thinking of getting him up to walk. We would be better off if we led with the story that there might be a rise in the subway fare. That's going to affect eight million people—the whole city!"

"We've been beating that story around since Thursday," Stephan argues. "It's an old story."

Stephan believes that the first story should be like the first line of a short story or the first chapter of a book. "You've got to interest the audience," he says. "Otherwise they'll shop around for other stations for the news."

Sometimes Ralph changes Stephan's mind. Today, he does not.

After Anna finishes writing her story, she stops in the wire service room to see if there are any **updates**—new information—on tonight's stories. Then she goes down to the sixth floor to get ready for the show. Her first stop is the makeup room. When she arrives, makeup artist Frances Kolar has already begun working on Ralph's face.

Stephan believes the first story on any news show should grab the audience's attention. Having a reporter on the scene of a local news event as it occurs can generate the right kind of excitement.

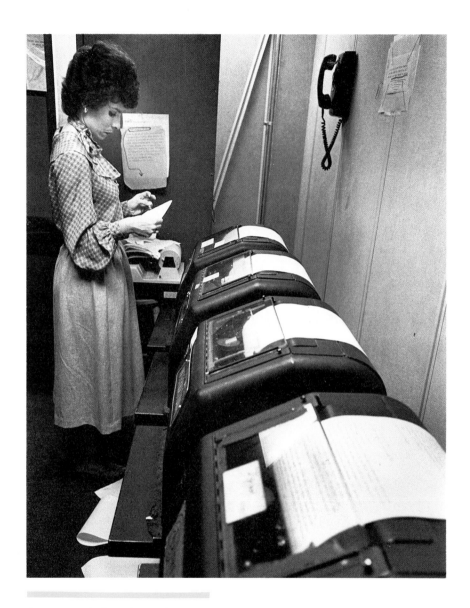

Anna stops in the wire service room
to check for news updates.

Even men wear heavy makeup under the strong lights of the TV camera.

Even men wear heavy layers of makeup when they are on TV. The strong lights can make some people look yellow or even green!

As Anna waits, she puts rollers in her hair. Anna and Ralph go on the air in twenty minutes—at 6:00 P.M.—but they chatter calmly. Beneath their coolness, however, there is tension. Anna is most nervous in these moments, right before going on the air. Anchors don't just read the news. They are also actors. They must sound serious when they read serious stories and cheerful for happier stories. "I have to put a lot of energy into being an anchor," Anna says. "It's like being on stage for a half-hour performance."

Soon it's Anna's turn to be made up. In front of Frances are many types of cosmetics and hair brushes. Frances works on Anna's face like an artist painting a picture. She uses brushes, sponges, and powder puffs. She rubs and pats and dusts her face with creams and powders.

When she's finished, Frances compliments Anna's blouse. Anna has an unusually large wardrobe. She keeps a calendar at home on which she writes down what she wears each day. She tries not to wear the same dress or blouse more than once every few weeks. TV audiences, she says, have a good memory—especially for what the anchor wears.

A young man sticks his head in the doorway. "We have eight minutes to the broadcast," he says cheerfully. He is Alan Goldfarb, the **stage manager.**

Anna quickly takes the curlers out of her hair and combs it.

"Five minutes to the broadcast," Alan says, passing

Makeup artist Frances Kolar
works on Anna's face as
though it were a painting.

by the door again. Ralph looks in the mirror and puts a few hairs back in place.

Before Anna leaves, Frances gives her a last pat with the powder puff. Powder helps prevent the hot lights from melting the makeup.

Next door to the makeup room is the **studio.** Dozens of lights hang from the ceiling. At one end of the room is the **set,** where the anchors sit. Ralph is going over his script, timing himself as he silently practices it one more time. Anna takes her seat, faces the cameras, adjusts the earpiece in her right ear, and clears her throat. Ralph attaches his microphone to his tie and Anna takes a last look in the mirror.

As they prepare for the cameras to roll, Ralph and Anna make some final adjustments to their equipment and Anna checks herself a final time in the mirror.

The stage manager's job is to **cue,** or give signals to, the anchors. Alan tells Anna and Ralph how many seconds are left before they're on the air. And when they're on the air, he uses his fingers to show them how many seconds they have left to talk. Alan knows what to tell Anna and Ralph because he is wearing an earpiece that connects him with the **control room.**

The man in charge of the control room tonight is Harry McNeill, the **director.** "The producer gives you all the ingredients and the director puts it all together," Harry explains. During the half-hour show, Harry constantly watches the twenty TV screens in front of him. They show the tapes that are coming up on the show, the different camera angles in the studio, and the many maps and special pictures that will appear on the show.

Harry is responsible for making sure that every part of the show appears on the viewer's TV screen at the right time. He tells the technical director, who sits to his right, when to change cameras and when to **roll,** or start, a tape. He also cues the audio director when it is time to start the music, and tells the lighting director when to turn on the studio's lights. The associate director, Sid Vassall, who sits on Harry's left, makes sure that the supers appear at the proper time and keeps track of how much time is left to the show. Without him, Alan would not know what to tell Anna and Ralph.

The control room, with director
Harry McNeill (middle), swings
into action as the show begins.

Harry must make decisions in a second. If equipment breaks down, if a reporter's voice cannot be heard
when he or she is on "live," Harry has to decide instantly
what to do. Sometimes, the control room gets very noisy
with everyone yelling and jumping out of their seats.

"Stand by, folks," Harry says, at a minute before six
o'clock.

"Thirty seconds; stand by."

Stephan sits behind Harry. He has a telephone that connects him with Anna and Ralph. He can also talk into their earpieces. One reason he may need to speak to them is to tell them about sudden changes in the script.

Harry leans forward in his seat.

"Lights. Stand by, camera one. Take it!"

The music begins, and a view of Channel 4's studio with Anna and Ralph appears on TV screens around the city.

"Take Anna on camera three," Harry says.

Now, only Anna's face can be seen on the screen. "Big lame duck sessions coming up in Albany and Washington this week," she says. "Both can affect your money . . . A big crafts show opens for holiday shoppers looking for something special . . . And the Giants do it again in the Meadowlands . . . they beat the Houston Oilers. Don Gould will have all the sports."

The words come out smoothly. Anna doesn't have to worry about memorizing them. In front of her, attached to the camera, is a **teleprompter,** which is a screen with all of tonight's stories written on it. Alan stands next to the teleprompter so that Anna can see his cues out of the corner of her eye.

Viewers enjoy watching Anna because they feel as though she's talking to them personally. How does Anna do that? "When I look in the camera," she says, "I think of people who *really* like me. I make believe I am talking to my family or the people I grew up with who are saying, 'Here's our Anna, telling the story.'"

Viewers like Anna because she is comfortable on camera and seems to be talking directly to them.

During the commercial, Anna and Ralph study their scripts. Don Gould takes his place on the set next to Ralph. There is a relaxed atmosphere in the studio. Alan is trying to think of a song from *The Wizard of Oz,* and Anna and Ralph try to help him.

But suddenly, Alan hears the director talking to him through his earpiece.

"In one minute, we're back on the air . . ."

The makeup artist dashes into the studio and blots Anna's lipstick. She's been watching from the control room and thinks it looks too shiny.

Alan takes his place next to the camera.

"We start on camera three. Here we go. In fifteen seconds we roll. Ten, nine, eight, seven . . ." At "one," Anna is on.

The show goes smoothly. A few minutes before the end, Anna hears Stephan's voice in her ear. "We're heavy by ten seconds." That means that the show took a little longer than he expected. When Stephan tells her it is "light," there is extra time. Since it is heavy tonight, Anna and Ralph will have to say good night quickly to their TV audience.

Upstairs in the newsroom, Anna meets her parents. They have a light snack in a nearby ice cream parlor and then Anna goes back to do the eleven o'clock show.

By the time it is over, Anna is tired. At home, she looks in on her sleeping child and then calls her hus-

band. She and her daughter will fly to Houston in a few days.

Tomorrow, Anna Bond will become a reporter again. Although she's done it hundreds of times before, she's not at all tired of her job. "I like what I do. I'm excited by it. I guess it's always a challenge to make people care— care about what's happening in the world around them, and most important, care about other people."

**GLOSSARY**

**anchor**—the person who reads the news and shows segments taped earlier by reporters.

**assignment editor**—the person who decides, with the producer, which stories will be reported and assigns reporters to cover them.

**audio technician**—the "sound" person. Records interviews and other sounds on location.

**control room**—the place where the director and other people involved in producing the show sit.

**cue**—a signal from the stage manager that tells the anchor when to start talking and how much time is left in a show.

**director**—seated in the control room, the director is the "boss" during the newscast, giving directions to technical, audio, and assistant directors and making sure that different scenes from a program appear on the TV screen at the right time.

**editing**—the process of selecting and combining the portions of videotape that will appear on the air.

**editing room**—the room containing the editing equipment, which allows the editor to edit the tape and create voice-overs.

**feature story**—a story, often with "human interest," that is not about a news event.

**kicker**—the last story in a news show.

**lead**—the first story in a news show.

**news story**—a story about an event that has just happened that day.

**producer**—the person who decides which stories will be on the program and how long each will be.

**roll**—the command given by a director to start taping.

**script**—a written version of the newscast.

**set**—the part of the television studio, seen on TV, in which the anchors sit.

**shotgun microphone**—a microphone used to pick up distant sounds.

**shots**—the pictures that appear on the TV screen.

**sound bite**—an interview.

**stage manager**—working in the studio, the stage manager sends cues and directions from the control room to the anchors.

**studio**—the room from which a TV show is broadcast.

**supers**—the names at the bottom of the TV screen that identify who is talking.

**tape page**—a piece of paper that tells precisely when an interview is due to appear on the screen. Used to inform technicians when to put supers on the screen.

**teleprompter**—a TV screen, attached to the studio camera, from which anchors read what they say on the air.

**time code**—numbers that appear on a TV screen in the editing room, indicating an exact place in the tape.

**updates**—new information about a news story.

**voice-over**—the reporter's voice heard during the video (picture) portion of the story.

**wire services**—organizations that supply news stories from around the world to TV stations and newspapers.

INDEX